D0923654

THE
UNIVERSITY OF WINNIPEG
PORTAGE & BALMORAL
WINNIPEG 2, MAN. CANADA
DISCARDED

DISCARD

The Phoenix Living Poets

———◁◁◁◁◁◁▷———

THE SAD MOUNTAIN

Poets Published in
The Phoenix Living Poets Series

★

ALEXANDER BAIRD · ALAN BOLD
GEORGE MACKAY BROWN
JENNIFER COUROUCLI
GLORIA EVANS DAVIES
PATRIC DICKINSON · D. J. ENRIGHT
JOHN FULLER · DAVID GILL
J. C. HALL · MOLLY HOLDEN
JOHN HORDER · P. J. KAVANAGH
RICHARD KELL · LAURIE LEE
LAURENCE LERNER
CHRISTOPHER LEVENSON
EDWARD LOWBURY · NORMAN MACCAIG
JAMES MERRILL · RUTH MILLER
LESLIE NORRIS · ROBERT PACK
ARNOLD RATTENBURY
ADRIENNE RICH · JON SILKIN
JON STALLWORTHY
GILLIAN STONEHAM
EDWARD STOREY · TERENCE TILLER
SYDNEY TREMAYNE
LOTTE ZURNDORFER

PR
6055
.A7 S 2

THE
SAD MOUNTAIN

by

TOM EARLEY

CHATTO AND WINDUS

THE HOGARTH PRESS

1970

Published by
Chatto & Windus Ltd
with the Hogarth Press Ltd
42 William IV Street
London W.C.2
★
Clarke, Irwin & Co. Ltd
Toronto

SBN 7011 1613 7

All rights reserved. No part of this publication may be
reproduced, stored in a retrieval system, or transmitted, in
any form, or by any means, electronic, mechanical, photo-
copying, recording or otherwise, without the prior permission
of Chatto and Windus Ltd.

© Tom Earley 1970

Printed in Great Britain by
T. H. Brickell and Son Ltd
The Blackmore Press, Gillingham, Dorset

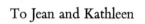
To Jean and Kathleen

Acknowledgements

Some of these poems originally appeared in *Anglo-Welsh Review*, *Poetry Wales*, *London Welshman*, *Outposts*, *Tribune*, *Country Quest*, *Breakthru*, *Poet* and *Second Aeon*.

Some appeared in the following anthologies: *Poetry for Peace* (Breakthru), *The Lilting House* (Dent-Davies), *Poems 69* (Gwasg Gomer), *Doves for the Seventies* (Corgi) and *A Storm of Bloods* (Second Aeon). A number were included in *Welshman in Bloomsbury* (Outposts), others were read and discussed on BBC programmes and one, *Too Soon*, was specially commissioned by the Welsh Arts Council for transmission on their *Dial a Poem* service.

Contents

Lark	*page*	9
Summer Return		10
Cwmpennar		11
The Tip Wood		12
Ram		13
Too Soon		14
Shadows		15
The Last Time		16
Japanese Rice Weed		17
Jackdaw		19
Search Yourself		20
Requiem		21
The Rocking Stone		22
Autumn in Wales		23
Mountain Ash		24
The Hills Are Wild Again		25
Rebirth		26
To a Professional Poet		27
Tiddlers		28
Welsh Girl's Voice		29
Ecumenical Catechism		30
Deep Dyffryn		31
Pictures in the Papers		32
When Morning Comes		33
The Tip Above Mountain Ash		34
Christian Unity in Wales		35
Return in April		36
Ffrwd Cemetery		37
The Moorhen Pond		38
Craig Y Dyffryn		39
Colours		40

Lark

Helicopter of the hill,
with your vertical take-
off and controlled poise
as you climb, you make
the mountain shrill
with your noise.

Coming in to land,
you drop suddenly
straight as a stone
to meet the ground
but not directly
to your home.

You leave the air
through cold couch-grass
and wind-blown heather
so none know whether
you merely pass
or live there.

If put to the test
when I was young,
I could find the nest
of any species among
the birds of Wales
except yours.

Summer Return

On this first August afternoon
I have climbed to the rocking stone
And now, at the summit of my summer,
I lie alone on a sprung bed
Of winberry bushes, looking down
Beyond the scrubby heather, beyond
The moss-covered tips and the clumping
Bracken to the mountain-sheltered town.

I watch the toy bus swing up the valley
As it did yesterday when we followed
The line of the river, the coaly Cynon
Black and shiny as a pair of Sunday shoes.
Its slaggy bank had been transformed
By masses of luxuriant ragwort,
Rosebay, hemp-agrimony and tansy
Into a mauve and yellow hedge.

As we approached the Penrhiwceiber pit
I noted again how the mountain
Had reached right down into the street
In a thickly covered slope of heather,
Bringing to Tynte a temporary loveliness,
To Ynysboeth an unexpected beauty,
And suddenly I saw the grassy tump
Of Twynbrynbychan dominate the town.

I looked up at the rocking stone
Which told me I would climb up here
Today and here I am now, satisfied
And lying at ease on my bouncing
Spring-mattress of a winberry bed,
Looking down at the familiar places
In mountain-sheltered Mountain Ash
On this first August afternoon.

Cwmpennar

This silent pit,
relinquished by men, has been reclaimed
by nature. There are willows now
in the waste land of the colliery yard;
they shake their shining catkins through
the gutted windows of the lamp room's shell.
The spicy tang of bracken blends
with permanent and pungent smell of coal.
The silver birches huddle closer
and stand like weeping women round the shaft.

All that remains
are two gaunt wheels that cut the line
of hill, the wall-protected shaft,
the pit-head gear in trim, the winding engine
at the ready: for just one man who must
go down each day to drive the pump and deal
with all the mountain water that collects;
its weight would break down the dividing wall
that separates it from Deep Dyffryn,
a pit where men are working day and night.

Deep down below
this yard now overgrown and green,
the pumping station, like an anchored
ship abandoned in the night with all
its crew except the captain gone, remains
an isolated relic dimly lit
surrounded by the water and the dark.
Beneath this tangled wilderness and wood
where boys are playing in the sunshine
a man is working under ground, alone.

The Tip Wood

A strange sensation I felt there
Waiting in the quiet autumn wood
Sheltered by the man-made mountain
Of blue coal soil and purple slag.

Not that it was just beautiful
To the eyes with the multi-coloured trees
Projected up against the blue-black tip
But it was also the silence and the sounds.

Faint rustling sound of soft fall of leaf
And sudden silence after staccato plop
Of acorn dropping or loose wind-killed twig
On to the dry brittle carpet of the wood.

As though the trees were waiting with me
For the final act, the final definitive act.

Ram

Saddle and shoulders royally marked
with purple dye, rain-clean wind-ruffled
beard flashing white against November gold,
this beautiful lean beast advances
across the cleared-green fenced-in island
in a copper-coloured sea of bracken
to where the still and patient ewes
willingly await their unfamiliar guest.

He holds his fine head high, with its
profile of aristocrat, eyes of dissipated rake,
ears half hidden by the dark eccentric crown
which curls like a shining cast in bronze
of a sculptured pair of giant snails.
Majestically he moves among his dull harem
choosing, discarding; lingers at this one,
half mounts, decides against it and descends.

Suddenly he sees between the barbed wire
an exotic stranger, her back and loins
stained scarlet, marked member of an alien
flock, putting herself forward to meet him.
She stops still as a statue except
for the quiver of her nostrils working like his.
They stand staring in a stupid sexual trance;
now he would jump the barrier if he could.

Just like a man, like every man
since Adam took the apple, like all
our vacillating trapped-in tribe
irresolute before the forked dilemma,
seeking fulfilment where it can't be found,
permanently striving for something else,
creating our own desires, never satisfied,
always wanting the one over the wall.

Too Soon

The February wind from the east
Had emptied the park of people
In spite of the unaccustomed sun.

The lovers walked beside the ruffled lake
Which lay suddenly as silent as when
A dabchick has dived and disappeared.

There was no sign of spring and the wind
Had made their noses permanently wet,
Their frozen faces ugly with the cold.

Then as they turned before the bridge
They saw them, embroidered on green,
The mauve and yellow crocuses under the trees.

But none of them were open to the sun.
Each one was closed against the bitter cold
As tightly as a sudden angry fist.

When later underneath the darkened trees
He tried to hold her warmly in his arms,
Her obstinate body remained stiff.

Her lips were unrelaxed, her heart
Tight fisted as the stubborn crocuses,
Cold as the February wind.

Shadows

The lantern's light projects
two intersecting shadows
from the sombre rafters
on the whitewashed stable wall.
An unmarried mother lies
in an improvised bed,
holding her crying child
in her inexperienced arms.
A man who feels out of place
watches silently from the darkness.
He sees the sweat on her face,
a stain of blood on the straw.
The light flickers again
and the shadows take shape.
Over the manger hangs a cross.

The Last Time

Although I have not climbed
This hill before, I remember
Every detail of it well:
The conflict at the start,
(You thought you had resolved it long ago)
The foreboding on the way up,
(You ought to have replaced your fear by love)
The unaccountable malaise at the top.
I do not want to climb
This hill again.

Although 1 have not found
This house before, I remember
Every detail of it well:
The brutish guard at the door,
(You have to be signed-in)
The religious maniac on the stair,
(You are required to know the pass-word)
The final and frightening confrontation.
I do not want to find
This house again.

Although I have not seen
This face before, I remember
Every detail of it well:
The fact that it has no ears,
(You have to speak with the sounds in your head)
The realization that it has no tongue
(You try to read the question in the eyes)
The triumphantly malevolent expression.
I do not want to see
This face again.

Japanese Rice Weed

We could have called it the Welsh rice weed,
Ubiquitous as it is in Wales,
Colouring the coaly banks of all
The black and shining rivers with prolific
Green, sheltering with its foliage the pale
Exotic lilac of the balsam flower,
The deeper purple of the willow herb.

But the pea-shooter plant we named it
As boys, breaking it down with our boots
And cutting our fancied length of tubing
From its bamboo-sectioned stem, which nature
Had already hollowed out and left
The perfect thickness for our ammunition
Of autumn-reddened berries from the thorn.

When we were here last in high summer
It stood broader than a man and higher,
Stood jungle-thick, its elongated smooth
And polished limbs blotched as with blood,
Its heart-shaped leaves hardly distinguishable
From those of its parasite, convolvulus,
Whose frail white bells were tangled in its stem.

Now at this searing end of winter
We see these relics of the last year's crop,
Dwarfed heaps of dead and whitened stalks
Cut down by frost and thrashed by bitter wind;
Yet underneath these dry and brittle sticks
Are curled-up crimson shoots waiting to thrust
Into a straighter and a stronger growth.

SM-B

We could have called it the Welsh rice weed
For at this time it symbolises Wales
Awakening from its sleep; these virile spikes,
Ready to replace the withered stumps, are like
The young emergent Wales preparing to break free
From all the alien clutter of the recent past
To struggle, a new nation, into life.

Jackdaw

Mischievous, they say, as a monkey,
Thieving as a magpie, meddlesome
As a child of two, but I have never
Found you so. The most I've seen
You take was wool for your nest
From a cud-chewing, complacent sheep.
I find you well-behaved and wonder
How your evil reputation arose.
I've never known your kind in England;
There you would seem alien, out of place.
But here in this mining village I see
Your relatives in all the streets, one pair
To every chimney. What do you eat
In this hungry place? Do you live on smoke?
I've seen you on the mountain, perched
On the back of a consenting ewe,
Picking tics from her fleece. But here
It's either the crumbs from the poor
Man's table or the flies. Normally
A quiet bird with your occasional
Low monosyllabic unraucous caw,
When you quarrel with your wife
You stand across your chimney pot
Like an eloquent Welsh preacher
Leaning out of the loud pulpit
In the holy passion of his *hwyl*.
Then I can well believe you could
Be taught human speech and I know,
Monoglot, that you would speak Welsh.

Search Yourself

Admonitory notice search yourself
confronts the collier at the pit-head gate
such metaphysical advice
in theologically erudite Wales
search yourself Laertes know thyself
to thine own searched-out self be true
replace Polonius by the psycho-analyst
you on the couch there search yourself
what were you thinking what your motives when
and you young miner crossing the colliery yard
have you searched not only your pockets but your self
your life what doing with it where going when
where whither wherefore and especially why
because why is a philosophical question.

Requiem

Mourn for the children who in earth are laid
And let us not forget that they were killed
By that sad mountain which their fathers made.

That tip had made tough miners feel afraid
And they, whose darkest fears have been fulfilled,
Mourn for the children who in earth are laid.

The price of coal has finally been paid
With those young bodies violently stilled
By that sad mountain which their fathers made.

Bereaved believing parents, who have prayed
Not to think this an act that God had willed,
Mourn for the children who in earth are laid.

They cannot face the future undismayed
In contemplating all they must rebuild
By that sad mountain which their fathers made.

And workers, who have often been betrayed,
Whose lives again with bitterness are filled,
Mourn for the children who in earth are laid
By that sad mountain which their fathers made.

The Rocking Stone

A stillness everywhere,
The Merthyr mountain bathed in golden light,
I stood above the stile
And waited for the sun to set again.
The Aberaman ponds were pools of blood,
The Brecon beacons black and jagged lines
Across the afterglow.

And darkness fell before I reached the stone,
A night with navy sky.
I sat against the ruined engine house
And listened to the noises from the town.
Above the mountain murmur of the Ffrwd,
The sadder sound of trucks
And sighing of the ventilator from the pit.

Autumn in Wales

Many kinds of metal glisten in the sun.
Copper leaves of beech now lighten to steel,
Now darken to bronze. Pinchbeck necklaces
Of elm sparkle above the chromium
Trunks of silver birch. Gold pieces
Of hazel and sycamore glitter against
The rusted iron of oak and fern or gleam
Between the obstinate summer-green of alder
And elder. Stubborn foxglove leaves still
Linger on the brown loam of the path
Through the bracken.
                                    But here the wood
Is windowed by diaphanous old man's beard
Which cannot hide the blood of autumn,
The red, endemic red of autumn, red
Of nightshade, hawthorn, bryony and rose.

Mountain Ash

The song of buckets on the aerial rope
And heart beat of compressor from the wood,
Sad hooter, shunting trucks' staccato tap,
Men's voices calling from the pit-head yard.

The hill's fine edge which cuts the afterglow
And high horizons stealing evening light,
A sky that's smaller, night that's all below
Dark walls of mountain black on either side.

The harvest moon above the valley slung
And slate roofs shining through the autumn haze,
Festoons of street lamps tracing patterned roads,
The moving pit-lamps of the night-shift men.

A London-lighted evening often brings
Such evocation of nostalgic things.

The Hills are Wild Again

Since television came
and people stay indoors
or only go to see
the country in their cars,
the strangeness of my step
has set the farm-dogs off
to bark in Gelliddu.

The sheep are hostile too,
the startled rams enraged.
The barking of the fox
can once again be heard
from distant mountain top.
The badgers have returned
below the Raven's Crag.
I have already seen
their circumstantial marks.

Tonight I must go out
and watch for them again
if only I can find
the way up in the dark
for hills are wild again
and footpaths in the wood
grown over and unused.

Rebirth

Because I have climbed the hill
I have delayed the sunset more than once.
Because I have climbed, the sun
That once had set
Has risen again in splendour
And flooded the mountain
With reflecting auburn light.

So now the hope I may
Delay that other setting,
The greying twilight of the mind,
Revives the thought of what
I'll gain from new ascension.
It will not be vain, I know now
Because I have climbed the hill.

To a Professional Poet

I sometimes think that you have said
it all, have spoken once for all
for all of us. You would perhaps
have disagreed with that.

'Listen to the sounds of the world
from outside you. Hear the echoes
of voices speaking to your heart
and singing in your head.

Know and feel all that is moving
around and within you. Then write
it down and work on it, shaping
shining over the year.'

As you did in your little shed,
working over your weight of words
fashioning and refashioning
as a good craftsman should.

Tiddlers

Here where the road now runs to Aberdare
the old canal lay stagnant in its bed
of reeds and rushes housing dragonflies
which flashed from sunshine into willow shade.

Beneath this very bridge we came to fish
for roach and perch and other smaller fry
like minnows, sticklebacks, and tiny frogs
and all these smelt peculiarly of pits.

A smell of stinkhorn-fungus, coal and damp
still clung to them as though they had swum up
some subterranean passage from the mine.

They smelt the house out when we got them home
and, when we changed the water, always died:
clean water killed them.

Welsh Girl's Voice

I listen to the way you intone
All this glowing Anglo-Welsh verse
Ranging all the width of your warm
Contralto voice, leaning on the stressed
Syllables with unnecessary weight.
A pianist could play
The tune you make
When you speak.

I look at your sensitive little face,
Illuminated, contrasting with the opaque
Blackness of your sad Welsh eyes,
As your voice begins to break
On one of Dylan's moving lines.
A pianist could play
The tune you make
When you speak.

But supposing that I were in love,
Were waiting by the unrewarding phone
And longing for your sympathetic voice
To heal the heartbreak of separation;
Then I know that I would not believe
A pianist could play
The tune you make
When you speak.

Ecumenical Catechism

Will those who with the holy roman walk
not drink but only taste the bitter cup,
joined merely in theology of talk,
not act but spend the time in making up?

Will pale horse running riderless away,
whose head was never held by rein nor cord,
distract our listening, when they have their say,
to south bank thinkers who disguise their lord?

Will ruthless light at last on us reveal
the mark of cain before we can atone,
our offering unaccepted, seventh seal
removed to show us what we should have known?

And shall we reap the grain devoutly grown
or gather tares that only we have sown?

Deep Dyffryn

Our town was headlined on the BBC,
Its pit, Deep Dyffryn, featured in the news.
No story of disaster, happily,

But only of two colliers having words
And using language, as we say in Wales;
Not so remarkable for men in mines.

The name Deep Dyffryn turns my memory
To boyhood days when I was envious of
My father working in this colliery.

He would not recognise the pit-head yard
Now it's become electrified and still.
In those days it was busy, bold and loud,

A restless hive, alive with urgent steam.
I still can hear the winding-engine's song,
The stamp of horse, the clatter of the tram,

The saw-mill's whining and the anvil's clang.
The ventilator seemed a living thing,
A giant snoring through his iron lung.

Pictures in the Papers

Bewildered girl, her vulnerable face
reflecting nightmare war, her little hand
in bloodstained bandage inexpertly dressed,
she limps along half leaning on a stick,
her wound ill bound in military haste,
parents already dead in battle wreck
of jungle town now named as Dong Xoai.

And sadder pictures that could make you cry:
grim soldiers shoot deserters in a ditch,
cold blooded, singly, while the others watch;
emaciated mother, staring wild
and streaming tears, enfolds her murdered child.

The poetry, he said, is in the pity.
We need another Wilfred Owen now.

When Morning Comes

Escaping the silent scream
Where the long night still lingers,
I wake from my remembered dream
Knowing again that my fingers
Were not able to loosen
The lock nor get the gate open.

Now sensing in the sullen gloom
That the new day's light is near,
No longer allowing room
For uncertainty or fear,
My mind accepts the fact that one
Cannot undo what has been done.

SM-C

The Tip Above Mountain Ash

I stood there on the shining tip, feeling
like flying over the grey slated town.
The air below was a glass bowl, was a clear pool
of Mellte water with magpies for fish, mute
mechanical magpies. As I stood there
above oblique Caegarw I marked again
their long-tailed clockwork flight like black
and white gigantic dragon-flies.

I stood there on the shining tip, hearing
the long Sunday-silence of the day,
hearing it broken again by the harsh morning
call of the vicarage rooks from the Maesydderwen
trees, by the pointless self-pitying cry of the grey
and shabby sheep from the Cefnpennar hill
where the winter sun was stirring the wet bronze
bracken and warming the trodden sheep-paths.

I stood there on the shining tip, staring
at straggling Darranlas across the toy
farm of Gelliddu and the working model
of Deep Dyffryn now silenced for Sunday
soon to be silenced for good and what then
I wondered will become of the lost towns
of Wales dearly beloved and cheaply betrayed
not by exiles only but by home-loving sons.

I stood there on the shining tip, thinking
of the old days of Wales and its people now
(while choirs disband and chapels close, replaced
by drinking club and bingo hall) caring for cars
but having for their language and literature
a cold and calculated indifference.
I looked at the magpies and listened
to the sheep and wondered about Welshmen.

Christian Unity in Wales

Our chapels all refuse to be united,
A new attempt would cause an awful row
And only make the deacons get excited
So let's keep off that controversy now.

Instead, it would be relatively easy
To join up with the people in the church
As long as we do not become too queasy
At leaving other chapels in the lurch.

We know the church is just the Tory party
At prayer, as someone has so rightly said,
We know their singing's not exactly hearty,
Not coming from the soul but from the head.

Yet we have faults and they must be admitted
Though at the moment I can't think of one.
Perhaps some little sin we have committed
Some charitable act we've left undone.

But not enough to give them cause to blame us.
Some formula could certainly be found.
And nonconformist tolerance is famous
As once I heard a minister expound,

"To live and let live is the only fair way.
We chapel men regard the church like this:
They only try to worship God in *their* way;
We only try to worship Him in *His*."

Return in April

The cool willow catkins and the burning
Yellow gorse welcomed me home to Wales.
That was yesterday when I arrived.
Impressions of the journey up the valley
Are fresh in my mind to memorize.

The bus was lurching, like an over-careful
Drunk, to miss the straying sheep; the driver
Had to stop and wait while little harrassed
Ewes crossed the road with their china lambs.

And then a zig-zag course avoiding loads
Of coal dumped in tidy heaps by certain
Chosen houses on both sides of the street.
The loads seemed smaller than they did.
No Easter bonus here, except for me:

The slow black river was sparkling in the sun
Like a stream of shining tar; above its banks
The cool willow catkins and the burning
Yellow gorse welcomed me home to Wales.

Ffrwd Cemetery

Even the sheep are frightened of this place.
With horror-haunted eyes,
They start and scramble off as though
They felt some presence near.
And yet they could not notice how
These tarnished headstones tilt at such
A terrifying angle to the town.

Since yesterday the skeleton has moved.
Still crouching here across
The overhanging dry stone wall,
Tonight it turns its skull
Away from mountain things. In mood
Of meditation, it appears
To contemplate the houses down below.

Perhaps the others have been here before,
All leaning on their stones,
Looking with saddened faces at
The darkening streets, as though
They disapproved of what they saw.
Get back into your graves and let
Us lead our lives the only way we know.

Since yesterday the skeleton has moved.
Who touched this unclean thing?
Perhaps some children from the town
Have dared to loose its limbs
And posture them a different way.
Strange how these white abandoned bones
Of mountain sheep so fascinate the young.

The Moorhen Pond

This lake was clean (we used to swim in it once)
and so clear that one could see under water
but in the centre it was deep and dark;
legend said it was bottomless, perhaps
an old shaft or a rock-fault common in Wales.

Around the edges there were rushes, reeds
and willows which provided nesting sites;
sometimes we could reach the nests by wading
but had more often to swim out for them.

Since they built the phurnacite plant, things
are different: the willows killed, the coot and moorhen
gone, the water covered with a thick black scum.

But there are fish in it still: red-finned roach
and stickleback, drab and dirty as the pond.

Welsh fish are not fussy.

THE
UNIV... DISCARD WINNIPEG
WINNIPEG 2, MAN. CANADA

Craig Y Dyffryn

The tips have priority now.
Some are suspect and must be made safe,
Scooped out and levelled by a giant's hand.
They are moving the Craig, more of a wood
Than a tip, covered with birch trees
And almost impenetrable undergrowth.
Harebells grow among the rough grasses
Of its summit and I have seen
A weasel snaking his long body
Through the sheltering brambles at its foot.
Now bumbling yellow bulldozers crawl
And clamber obstinately across the steep
Sides of the tip, blunder through the birches
Like ungainly dinosaurs, lumbering,
Crashing down the trees, tearing giant handfuls
Of the woods, where we picked blackberries
And gathered water cress. All the birds,
From magpie to the long-tailed tit, have gone.
The celandines and wood anemones
Already have been torn up by the roots.
There will be no bluebells this year, no
Branches for the honeysuckle to climb,
No foxgloves in the fullness of the summer.
The tips have priority now.

Colours

The valley's white, white with its tumbling brooks
And pigmy rapids polishing the stone
In frothy streams that slide down slippery rocks
To lose identity in Cynon's flood.

The valley's grey, grey with its threadbare sheep,
Gaunt shabby rams that wait in autumn wood,
Thin haggard ewes that scrounge the winter street
And fragile lambs that freeze in April wind.

The valley's black, black with endemic slag
In tips of ever changing silhouette,
Where, like a funeral, trucks in mourning go
Reflected in the river's tarry shine.

Yet when in absence I evoke the scene
The colour of the valley's always green.